SECOND BASE

MASTERY

Dominating the Diamond

The Complete Second Baseman

Skills, Strategies, and Leadership

SKY BENSON

TABLE OF CONTENTS

CHAPTER 1

FUNDAMENTALS OF SECOND BASE

Understanding your role

"And responsibilities"

Second base is not a position requiring a single player's spectacular plays or heroics. When it comes to the infield, it is about having a firm hand on the rudder and quiet competence. It is about being the player your teammates can rely on, the one who can comprehend the delicate dance that is second base and perform it beautifully. However, to achieve dominance over the diamond, you must first have a solid understanding of the core of your role, which consists of the critical capabilities that characterize the position.

In the infield, the most critical asset

The essential job that falls on your shoulders is successfully collaborating with the shortstop to create the "keystone combination." Within the infield defense, this alliance serves as the core foundation. You are the gatekeeper and accountable for everything that is hit between first and second base. Additionally, you are liable for behind throws to first base. There are a variety of ground balls, blazing line drives, and tricky pop-ups that fall under your purview. This does not mean that you are an isolated island, however. Working together is essential. You and your shortstop need to be on the same page, anticipating each other's actions and communicating like a well-oiled machine to be successful. It is essential to be aware of your partner's positioning and intentions to enable seamless execution of any move, whether it be a force play at second or a double play turn.

When it comes to the art of double-play

The mastery of the second base is crowned with the crown jewel of turning two. The rapid throws, exquisite footwork, and immaculate communication are all part of the symphony that is this event. You need to be confident in your ability to field the ball, make a lightning-fast transfer to the shortstop, and then release a precise throw to first base to get out of the game. This dance involves a lot of complexity, but if you can master it, you can completely change the course of a game. The double play is not solely about one's physical capabilities. It needs thinking strategically. Knowing when to prioritize the force out at second or when to attempt the double play is a skill that requires you to have an understanding of events. Anticipating bunts and rollers becomes much more critical when runners are on the bases. Reading the batter and the scenario can decide whether a routine out is converted into a double play that changes the course of the game.

The Double Play: Beyond the Double Play

It is not the only obligation that falls on your shoulders, even though the double play is the ultimate goal. Additionally, you are the first line of defense against bases that have been stolen. To discourage runners, covering the bag and making powerful throws at home is vital. Even in this case, anticipation is an essential factor. If you can read the indicators that the pitcher is giving off and anticipate the runner's jump, you will have the advantage you need to throw them out. Being sure to field routine ground balls should not be overlooked. When misplayed, a play that appears to be straightforward might become a costly misstep. By becoming proficient in glove work, footwork, and throwing mechanics, you can ensure that you won't miss any easy outs and will maintain control of the game.

In-field leadership entails

When you play second base, it's not only about your performance; it's also about contributing to the overall improvement of your playing field. You are the quarterback of the infield, and it is your responsibility to direct your teammates and call plays. You must be a vocal leader who maintains everyone's focus and communicates efficiently, particularly with your partner who plays shortstop. You can think of it as the conductor of an orchestra. In the same way, that the conductor directs the musicians to produce harmony, you need to direct your infield to create a masterpiece of defensive play. You, as the second baseman, are responsible for conducting the defensive symphony made by a well-coordinated infield capable of shutting down hostile offenses.

Introducing the Unsung Hero

Even though the second baseman might not be the one to hit home runs or make spectacular catches in the outfield, their duty is just as crucial, if not more so. You are the quiet protector of the infield, the one who ensures that every ground ball is fielded, every throw is sent toward its intended target, and every double play is turned.

The basis upon which you build your mastery of second base is getting a good understanding of your function and the obligations that come with it. Developing into a well-oiled machine, a player your teammates can trust, and a leader who confidently commands the infield are all critical aspects of this endeavor. Acknowledge the responsibility that comes with it, work on improving your talents, and become the player who quietly controls the game from second base.

Perfecting your fielding stance

"And techniques for ground balls."

The second base is known as "ground ball central" for a reason. Many of your defensive fights will be against rockets that bounce and scream immediately. The most important thing for a great second baseman is learning to catch ground balls. On the dirt, this is where your defense skills shine. What does it take to become a ground ball gobbler? It all starts with getting better at your catching stance and moves. Here is a list of the most important things that will make you a ground ball magnet.

The Base: The Ready Position

Your ready position is like your home base for defense. It's where you start every time you go after a ground ball. The important thing is to be at ease, keep your balance, and be ready to act immediately. Your knees should be bent a little, and your feet should be shoulder-width apart. Picture yourself in a low, muscular crouch, ready to jump. Keep your center of gravity low. This will let you move faster in any direction. Your weight should be spread out evenly between both feet to make a stable base. Now it's your turn. Hold your arm out before you, just below your belt buckle. Fingers loose but ready to wrap around the ball.

Your other hand should be on the side of the Glove closest to your throwing hand. This will give you more support and help you follow the ball's path. Don't forget to keep your eyes on the ball and your head down. It may not make sense to do this, but it lets you respond naturally to the hop and direction of the grounder. Trust your side vision to see baserunners and other things that might happen during the game.

Footwork: The Dance of the Ground Ball

If you hit the ball, your feet will play the game. You need to get good at your footwork to quickly field ground balls of any speed or direction. As the ball is hit, take a small shuffle step with the foot that isn't being shot toward the ball. This points you in the right direction and lets you know how far away something is. This is called "The Plant." As you get closer to the ball, firmly plant your front foot to make a stable base for catching. This is where you "attack" the ball on the ground. Use a crossing step if the ball hops or changes direction without you expecting it to. To quickly move your weight and change your playing position, step your back foot across your front foot. Once you've caught the ball, you change your footwork to start throwing. To make a strong throw, take a small hop step with your back foot toward your target, which is usually first base.

You can trust Glove's work as a partner.

When it comes to ground balls, your Glove is your tool. Make a funnel with your Glove as the ball gets closer. The netting must be closed as the ball enters the Glove to ensure a clean catch. To catch low grounders, put your Glove under the ball, use your legs and body to control the hop, and bring the ball into your playing pocket. Don't forget about the backhand! To catch a ball hit to your left side, smoothly turn your body and Glove to the backhand side. Keep the hand low and slightly angled inwards to make space for the ball.

Getting Good at Different Ground Balls

Not every ground ball is the same. You need to be gentler with these tricky devils. Focus on a controlled fielding move instead of a hard throw as you kneel and smother the ball with your Glove. For screamers that hug the ground, stay low, Glove down, and be firm, ready to block the ball instead of catching it neatly. These need to be planned out and timed. To make a smooth catch, hop and jump just enough to meet the ball at its peak.

Making Practice Better

It takes hard work and practice to get good ground ball skills. Have a partner hit your ground balls from different angles and distances to work on your footwork and glove work. Use a ground ball machine to simulate game-like situations with balls going in various speeds and directions. Do fielding drills with your feet and stance without a ball, focused on moving smoothly and reacting quickly. Repetition is the key to getting things done. The more you do these moves, the more they become part of your muscle memory. As a result, you'll act automatically, changing every ground ball into an easy out. You can change from chasing ground balls to gobbling them by getting better at catching stance, footwork, and getting a feel for your Glove. Remember, though, that the equation isn't just about physics.

Getting more aware of your surroundings

Ground balls aren't just thrown around. Pay attention to the batter's stance, how they hit, and the count. This can help you determine what kind of contact they're most likely to make (pull hitter, opposite-field grounder, etc.). Your strategy changes when there are runners on base. Even if the fielding isn't excellent, you might choose a faster throw to first for a force out. Talk to your shortstop and other infielders about possible double plays and who will cover the bag on a steal attempt.

How to Field Deeply

You don't just watch the area around the bag at second base. You should also be able to run deep into the right field to catch balls hit into the gap. "The Deep Approach" means taking a quick first step toward the ball when it is hit deep and then switching to a controlled run. To make quick changes of direction, keep your center of gravity low. You may need to use the backhand play if the ball is hit to your right side. Remember to keep your Glove low and angled inward to make a pocket when you use the backhand method. Talk to your right fielder as you range deep to avoid crashes, and ensure the play goes smoothly if they take over.

The Mind Game

When runners are on base, ground balls can be very annoying. Don't overthink about the play. Keep your eyes on the ball, act on instinct, and believe in your skill. Figure out how to do well when things get tough. Focus your worried energy on making the play with a strong will. Errors happen to everyone. Do not think about them too much. Pay attention, change how you do things, and keep an upbeat attitude on the field.

If you learn to field ground balls properly and keep your mind focused, you'll become a second baseman who makes hitters afraid. You're in charge of ground balls. Take charge of them and use them as outs. Your team will be able to count on you to defend them, and you'll be the quiet guardian of the infield and a master of the ground ball.

Developing quick

"And accurate throws."

Two things make or break a second baseman's image on the baseball field: how well they field the ball and throw it. You might be great at getting ground balls, but if you throw to first base like a drunk butterfly, you're not good at defense. Mastering quick, accurate throws is what makes a great second baseman and turns a good defender into a game-changer.

Putting the base together

To throw hard, you need to know how to do it right. Together, your body, arm, and hand move in a planned dance that gives you power and accuracy. How you hold the ball is critical. One of the best fastball grips for second basemen is a four-seam grip. This grip gives you reasonable control and makes it easy to let go. Place your thumb across the laces to stabilize the ball as it rests across the seams. Your windup should be small and work well. You can start to throw with a small crow-hop or a tiny turn. Don't forget that speed is more important than a full windup like a pitcher. Keep your arm up high and bent behind your head when you throw. This makes a spinning effect that gives the throw more power. Do not drop your elbow or loop your arm; this can make you less accurate. Take a small step forward with your front foot as you throw. Step 2: Step back as you throw. This helps you move your body weight into the throw and builds speed. Your arm doesn't give you all the power you need to throw. Focus on your core and shift your hips firmly toward your goal. This spinning power makes the throw stronger. Finish your throw with a strong follow-through after you let go of the ball. This ensures the fastest speed and helps keep accuracy.

The Art of Getting Out

The release point—where the ball leaves your hand—is significant for precision. When you use the same release point every time, the ball follows a known path, which makes it easier for your first baseman to catch it cleanly. Always throw the ball at the same height and angle, around your ear or slightly higher.

Getting faster at throwing

Second basemen need to be accurate, but their throws also need some zip. Strengthening your core, shoulders, and arms will help you throw farther. Rowing long distances with a person can help your arm muscles get more robust and flexible over time. Make sure that good mechanics come before raw force. As you do plyometric exercises like jump squats and box jumps, your explosive power will improve, which will help you throw the ball farther.

Getting good at different throws

There are more skills a second baseman can use than just throwing to first. You can use the underhand throw if you need to catch a runner taking bases. It is a quick throw that is used for short distances. Get out of a jam with the sidearm throw, which works best when runners are close to the base. To turn a double play, you must throw quickly and accurately to the shortstop for the pivot. You should practice this throw with your shortstop partner to ensure it goes smoothly.

Getting Better at Accuracy

Getting it right is just as important as speed, if not more so. Work on skills that help you improve your footwork. Good footwork gives you a stable base that lets you throw more accurately. Setting up targets at different distances is an excellent way to practice throwing the ball regularly to those targets. This helps your muscles remember what to do and makes you a better thrower. Having someone catch your throws lets you get feedback immediately, enabling you to improve your technique.

How to Think When You Throw

As a pitcher, you have to be able to throw under pressure. Don't let what's going on get to you. Pay attention to the techniques and believe in your training. Before you throw, picture yourself making a perfect throw. This upbeat thought can boost your confidence and help you do better. Everyone misses throws. Keep your mistakes in the past. Get rid of them, learn from them, and then play better the next time.

You'll go from being a timid thrower to a confident gunslinger at second base if you improve your arm strength, throwing mechanics, and accuracy. But technique and muscle memory aren't the only things that make throwing fun.

CHAPTER 2

TURNING TWO WITH PRECISION

Mastering the art

"Of the double play"

The two-for-one. Many athleticism, teamwork, and quick choices make up the symphony. The difference between good second basemen and great ones is what you see on highlight reels. Turning two isn't just about flashy plays; it's also about making a complicated defense move quickly and accurately. You need to do great on this test because it's the final test of your skills. Make sure you pass it.

What a double play is made of

The second baseman and the shortstop must work together for a double play to work. When the ground ball comes in, the second baseman catches it and quickly passes it to the shortstop covering second base. The shortstop turns their foot while keeping their body close to the base and throws the ball to the first baseman. When the throw comes in, the first baseman stops the runner coming from first base for the first out. This is an optional throw to home plate. If necessary, the first baseman could throw the ball to the catcher to tag out a runner trying to steal third for the second out.

The Job of the Second Baseman

You must play second base. It all starts with a good catch of the ground ball. Don't forget the basics: quick footwork, smooth glove work, and a good catch. The clock starts to run when you get the ball.

This is the transfer.

The most important part of the double play is the switch from your Glove to the shortstop's. Speed is critical. Every millisecond is essential, so the download must be lightning-fast. Try different transfer methods until you find one that feels easy and lets you go as fast as possible. A lousy pass can throw off the whole play. Try to get the ball right into the shortstop's hand for a smooth transition. Make a quick call to your shortstop, like "backhand," to let them know what kind of move you're making.

Double Play Changes

Every double-play is not the same. If the runner on first base has to go to second, getting the out at first base becomes the most important thing. Sometimes, you need to make a quick throw to first base, even if the move to shortstop isn't perfect. This is the standard double play: the shortstop turns and throws to first for the first out, and then there's a chance to throw home for the second out. This happens when one runner tries to steal second base and another steals third. A double play can occur if the second baseman tags the runner who is stealing second and throws home to catch the runner who is stealing third.

Getting along with your shortstop on double plays

Communication and working together are the most essential parts of a double play. Set aside time during practice sessions to do double-play drills only. Practice different situations, shifts, and ways to talk to people. Come up with a way to speak during double plays without yelling directions. This could be done through quick calls or hand signals. Does your shortstop excel at the backhand or the forehand? Do they like quick throws, or would they rather have more control? You can change your method if you know your shortstop's strengths and weaknesses.

Getting ready for the play and reading it

When playing second base, a good player doesn't just respond; they plan. Keep an eye on the batter's swing and how they hit the ball. You should be ready for a double play if they hit a hard ground ball toward the hole. Your strategy can be changed by the number of outs and the speed of the baserunners. A force play at second might be the better choice if there are two outs and a slow runner on first. If you see a chance for a double play, quickly tell your shortstop what you want to do (for example, "two!").

How to Think About the Double Play

When you turn two, you're bound to feel pressure. Don't let what's going on stress you out. Pay attention to the mechanics, believe in your training, and make sure you can talk to your shortstop easily. Imagine Succeeding: Picture yourself making a perfect move and a successful throw before a double play. This upbeat thought can boost your confidence and help you do better. Double plays don't always work. Do not focus on mistakes. Look at what went wrong, talk to your shortstop about it, and change how you play the next time.

How to Become a Double Play Machine

You can go from being a player in double plays to a double-play machine by getting better at fielding, mastering the art of transferring the ball, learning about the different types of double plays, and working together well with your shortstop. But it's not just about tools and working together.

Learning to do the double play is a process, not a goal. If you train regularly, talk to your shortstop, and work on improving, you will become a formidable defensive force. Every good double-play you make shows how dedicated you are and how well you know the keystone position. So, go out on the field with confidence and a strong desire to turn two. This will help you become the defense master of the double play.

Building chemistry

"With your shortstop"

When it comes to the baseball diamond, there aren't many partnerships that carry as much weight as the one between the shortstop and the second baseman. You are the gatekeepers between the pitcher and home plate, making you the most critical part of the infield. But without a strong connection, your defense is like a weak bridge - prone to crumble under pressure. To develop chemistry with your shortstop, it is not enough to simply like each other; you must also establish a telepathic connection with them so that they can smoothly play defense simultaneously. You may cultivate that winning connection by following these steps:

The importance of communication cannot be overstated.

Communication is one of the most important aspects of a successful cooperation between second base and shortstop. Create a system of hand signals or fast calls that can be used in multiple scenarios. Just saying "two!" before attempting to play a double play can make all the difference in the world. Please ensure you and your partner are on the same page by discussing these signs in advance. Learning to interpret each other's body language, in addition to pre-defined calls, is essential. If your shortstop gives a slight nod, it could indicate that he is prepared to throw backhand. Your indication to prioritize a force out could be as simple as sending a glance toward first base. Nonverbal communication can be as successful as verbal communication, particularly in circumstances requiring swiftness and quiet concentration.

The phrase "practice makes perfect" (and describes telepathy)

Try not to anticipate flawless teamwork in a single day. Make sure that your practice sessions are focused solely on developing your chemistry. Combine double-play drills, ground ball exercises, and basic throwing routines into your program. Your talents will be improved with each repeat, and you will also learn to anticipate your partner's moves as you progress through the exercise.

Get to know your partner's style.

In the same way, people have hands that they prefer to use; shortstops have a favorite method of throwing. Does your shortstop like to throw with their backhand, or do they feel more comfortable with a transfer with their forehand? Understanding their preferences enables you to modify your throws according to those preferences, which guarantees a seamless transition from your Glove to theirs.

Embrace the Accidents You've Made

When playing on the field, mistakes are unavoidable. However, how you deal with them might determine the nature of your partnership. Mistakes should not be allowed to become competitions of pointing fingers. Instead, after the play, you should discuss the scenario with one another, figure out what might have gone wrong, and adjust your strategy for the next time.

The phrase "beyond the field."

It is not just the diamond that is involved in building chemistry. On a more intimate level, you should get to know your shortstop. Participate in activities that bring you together away from the field, such as lunch or hanging out. This sense of camaraderie helps cultivate mutual respect and trust, ultimately resulting in improved communication and teamwork performance on the field.

Having a Passion for the Game That We All Share

Having a shared enthusiasm for baseball with another person is a great bonding agent. Conversations about players you admire, discussions about game plans, and even watching videos of spectacular defensive plays can be had together. This mutual enthusiasm fuels your motivation, making it more likely that you will both remain involved in mastering the skill of infield defense.

Celebrate your successes, no matter how big or how small

We are performing a double play that will conclude the game. Everyone should give each other high fives! Be sure not to undervalue the significance of recognizing even the most insignificant accomplishments. A well-executed throw to first base or a ground ball that is flawlessly fielded are both worthy of a pat on the back. Celebrating these victories, no matter how great or small helps to encourage positive teamwork and maintains a happy attitude.

It is a unit that you and your shortstop make up. Establishing an unbreakable keystone link can be accomplished by prioritizing communication, devoting practice time to one another, gaining knowledge of each other's techniques, and cultivating a solid friendship. What is the result? A force commanding defensively and instilling dread in the hearts of batters competing against them. Go forth, work on your chemistry, and make it your goal to become the most formidable pair of shortstops and second basemen on the field!

Quick transfers

"And avoiding the slide at second."

It's not enough to catch ground balls as a second baseman. It's cool to give the ball to your shortstop for a double play or a throw to first. Transferring the ball slowly can mean the difference between an out and a runner getting to base safely. To get good at the quick move and turn those grounders into outs, follow these steps:

Developing Method

It's essential to grip and rip the ball, not your Glove. Hold the ball firmly in your Glove, but not too tightly. A loose grip makes it easier to move and release the ball faster. Keep your Glove open and pointed inwards so the ball has a place to land. It's easier to pick up and move the ball quickly from this spot. "The Short Arm Throw" means to "flick" the ball instead of "throw" it. Do not waste time moving your whole arm. You should flick your wrist and elbow quickly instead of sending the ball to the shortstop. Picture the hand of your shortstop as a target. They should practice moving the ball to a particular spot in their Glove to make a clean catch with as little delay as possible.

Speed Drills

It takes practice to get better, and this time it's faster. Get a partner and have them hit your ground balls. Pay attention to making quick changes while staying accurate. Change sides with your partner so you can practice getting thrown to by them. With a ball in your Glove, stand before a mirror and pretend to catch ground balls. Focus on making your hand movement smooth and efficient as you practice the transfer motion at a breakneck speed. You'll not use it in a game, but training one-handed transfers can help your hand-eye coordination and transfer speed. Begin slowly and slowly speed up as you feel more comfortable.

Ability to be solid and bendy

Faster transfers are helped by having a solid core and flexible arms. You might want to add core strengthening routines and wrist stretches to your workout routine. More stable core stability lets you move with more control, and flexible wrists let you move your hands faster during the switch.

As I read the hitter

Being ready for the contact can sometimes give you an edge in the transfer. Keep an eye on the batter's swing and how they hit the ball. A quick underhand toss might work if they hit a weak grounder right at you. On the other hand, a hard-hit line drive needs a faster transfer with a little more speed.

Situations in games

Sometimes, you don't need a move to happen very quickly. If the runner on first base has to move to second, they must race to get out at first base. A quick move can save even a throw that is slightly off target. This is where speed shines. In a double play, every instant counts, so make sure you get to your shortstop quickly for a smooth play. When there are runners on base, it might be more critical for your shortstop to make a clean catch than the speed of the move. When this happens, you should focus on getting the ball and then make a controlled move.

"Don't Use the Slide at Second: Communication is Key"

For any second baseman, the slide can be the worst thing. A runner who doesn't follow the rules or has bad running skills can hurt you and throw off the play. Talk to them before the game. Tell them if they think there will be a steal attempt or a hard slide so you can be ready. Don't stand on the base right away. Move a little away from the bag. This will make the runner change their slide path, giving you more room to make the tag. If the runner is coming at you fast, a well-timed fake throw to first base can make them pause or change the direction of their slide, giving you valuable moments to make the tag. Do not be afraid to yell! An angry "Hey!" or "Slide here!" can wake the runner and tell them to slide carefully. Your safety is essential. If a runner is carelessly sliding toward first base, put your safety first and avoid getting caught in the slide. Talk to the referee and inform your team about how aggressive the runner is.

You can go from being an excellent second baseman to a great one by learning how to make quick moves, being aware of your surroundings, and using innovative strategies to avoid dangerous slides into a master of defense. With your speed and protective skills, you'll be the player who turns close plays into outs, gives your teammates confidence, and makes base runners afraid. Getting better at the keystone position is a process that never ends. Keep working on your transfer method, watch the game, and change how you play based on the batter and the runners on base. It won't be long before your second base defense turns into a fortress, showing your dedication to learning your craft.

CHAPTER 3

RANGE AND AGILITY

Exercises to increase

"Lateral movement and range"

As a second baseman, your defensive area is enormous. It's a place where you can be quick and move laterally. You need to be able to move quickly from side to side on the field to catch ground balls and stop steal attempts. But it takes time to get good at moving laterally. Here is a list of exercises that will help you improve your footwork and protective range:

Building the Base: Stability and Strength

For explosive side-to-side action, you need a strong base. Focus on building your core and lower body strength before moving on to more advanced drills. Planks, side planks, and Russian twists are all exercises that work your core muscles. These exercises keep you stable and in control when you move laterally. These workouts will make your quads, hamstrings, and glutes stronger. These are the muscles that make your side shuffle and jump so powerful.

Footwork Drills: How to Do the Shuffle

The second base slide is the move that you do best. This is the essential move for the Lateral Shuffle. Start with short, smooth shuffles to the side, ensuring your center of gravity is low. As you get better, slowly increase the distance and speed. This drill makes the knee lift bigger during the walk, which makes your hips more flexible and quicker. Keep your shuffle controlled as you bring your knees up to your chest. You can work on your balance with an agility ladder by doing in-and-out shuffles, carioca drills, and lateral lunges. The ladder gives you an apparent reference and helps you better at stepping correctly.

Adding Power to Your Movement with Explosive Drills

Begin by doing small side jumps, making sure you land softly and push off with your whole foot. Step by step, make the jumps farther and more powerful. You can test your leg strength and balance by jumping onto a box at a height you can easily reach. Get more vigorous as you go and move on to more giant boxes. Shuffling side-to-side over a set of low boxes is an excellent way to combine shuffling and hopping. This drill helps you get stronger and better coordinated to change directions quickly.

Exercises that use plyometrics

When you do plyometric exercises, you strengthen your muscles by training them to use their power in short bursts.

Squat Jumps: Squat down and jump as high as you can quickly. Softly land and do it again.

Depth Jumps: When you step off a stage at a safe height, jump as high as you can immediately. Softly land and do it again.

Always warm up before a workout to avoid getting hurt. Start slowly and build up the volume and difficulty of the drills over time. Pay attention to form over speed. You can work out the correct muscles with the proper form and avoid getting hurt. Adding lateral movement drills to your regular workout routine will help you improve over time.

Beyond Drills: Training Like a Game

Even though drills are essential to learn lateral movement, you should also train in ways that are similar to games:

Shadow receiving: Move from side to side, dive for fake balls, and practice throws to make it feel like you're receiving ground balls.

Partner Drills: Have a partner hit tennis balls on the ground, forcing you to react and slide to make plays.

Drills in the infield: Do full infield drills with your team. Representing game events helps you better move laterally when you're under pressure.

Do strength training

You might want to add pressure bands to your drills to move laterally. If you add some extra resistance, you can make your actions even more substantial and faster.

If you do these routines regularly and use game-like situations, you'll go from being a second baseman who doesn't move to one who is a master of lateral movement. You can defend yourself better because your range will grow, and your footwork will be perfect. Learning how to move laterally is an ongoing process. If you keep pushing yourself and eyeing good form, the second base area will soon feel like your playroom.

Anticipating hits

"And positioning yourself effectively."

You are not simply a fielder with a glorified position but a defensive strategist when you play second base. You have a secret weapon in the form of mastery of anticipation, which enables you to position yourself precisely before the ball is ever hit. Developing this priceless ability and becoming a defensive genius on the field can be accomplished by following these steps:

Be familiar with the hitter.

In the beginning, you will find the batter. Pay attention to their posture, their swing directions, and their average at the plate. A wide stance with their weight back may indicate that the player is a pull hitter who is most likely going for the right side of the field. There is a possibility that a closed stance and weight on the front foot indicate a line-drive hitter. A ground ball or a line drive may result from a rapid and compact swing. A lengthy and looping swing could produce a fly ball. Pay attention to the hitter's batting average and determine whether they tend to hit more fly balls, line drives, or ground balls. Make use of this information to anticipate being contacted by them.

Reading the Pitcher

A fastball is likelier to be struck, whereas an off-speed pitch may result in softer contact or pop-ups. Fastballs are more likely to be hit. The hitter may be swinging for the fences while the count is 0-2, which increases the likelihood that the ball will fly out of the park. Because the count is 3-2, they might be seeking to hit anything to get a base hit, which increases the likelihood that they will hit a ground ball. Is the pitcher more likely to throw within or outside the boundaries? This can put the hitter in a position to try to hit the ball.

Evaluation of the Current Predicament

Aside from the batter and the pitcher, when there are two outs, a ground ball can result in a double play, which should encourage you to position yourself somewhat closer to second base. This is because a double play can be a double play. The presence of baserunners has the potential to change your positioning. You may need to move closer to cover a possible theft attempt.

If you were to take your position

Given everything shown, it is time for you to assume your starting position. The standard position is a position that is slightly off the bag towards second base. It allows you to field ground balls, throw to first base, and pivot for the possibility of double plays. You may need to shift towards first or third base to anticipate certain types of hits. This will depend on the hitter as well as the circumstances. If you are altering positions, it is essential to convey your position to your teammates, particularly the shortstop. This will help you avoid confusion and ensure your defensive coverage is consistent throughout the game.

Adjusting Your Expectations to Fit the Situation

Having anticipation is a process that never ends. While watching games in the major leagues, pay attention to how professional second basemen position themselves and alter their movements differently depending on the circumstances. Every game is an opportunity to gain knowledge and experience. Immediately following each hit, examine your position and determine whether or not you could have predicted the play more accurately. Before each pitch, visualize the type of contact you anticipate and the ideal defensive posture in which you would like to position yourself. This mental repetition may heighten your anticipation.

This is not always the case with anticipation. At times, even the most skilled second basemen are taken by surprise. On the other hand, if you can become an expert at reading the hitter, pitcher, and game context, you can position yourself correctly and convert a more significant number of batted balls into outs. As a result, you will develop into a defensive chess master, constantly one step ahead of the batter and an essential component of your team's success. Keep gaining knowledge, continue to observe, and have faith in your gut feelings. You can turn yourself from a reactive fielder into a proactive defensive force ready to anticipate and defeat any hit that comes your way if you put in the effort to train and demonstrate dedication.

Handling pop-ups

"And line drives"

Ground balls are not the only thing played at second base; it is also about owning the entire airspace between first and second. It is necessary to have quick reflexes, excellent footwork, and a confident glove to perform pop-ups and line drives. Here is how you may go from being a person who enjoys gazing at the sky to being a fly ball maestro on the diamond:

Pop-Ups: Having Patience and Concentration

If you underestimate pop-ups, you could make mistakes, even if they appear easy outs. One of the most essential rules of pop-ups is to communicate clearly and concisely. When you see the ball appear, you should immediately call for it and let your teammates know what you intend to do. Confusion and probable crashes are avoided as a result of this. The pop-up should not be pursued. Move backward in a fluid manner while maintaining your focus on the ball. Strive to maintain a comfortable stance with your knees slightly bent and your Glove extended upwards towards the ceiling. While the ball is falling, alter the position of your Glove so that it is in contact with it at its highest point. Instead of making a spectacular diving grab, you should concentrate on cleanly capturing the ball. Making a secure catch is always preferable rather than missing an opportunity. As soon as you have secured the catch, you should prioritize creating a speedy transfer to your shortstop to potentially make a double play, or you should throw immediately to first base to record the out.

The Art of Tracking Line Drives

In defensive plays, line drives are the most exciting and exciting plays. Your undivided attention is required because they are quick, unexpected, and demand it. Pay attention to the speed of the bat and the path as it swings. It is common for a line drive to be indicated by a rapid and compact swing. React explosively with your first step. Taking immediate action is necessary for line drives. Ensure that your eyes remain fixed on the ball during its entire trajectory. Make sure you don't lose even a single second of concentration. Move your Glove such that it meets the course of the ball. Instead of reaching or lunging, the objective is to move in a smooth and controlled manner. In the context of "Playing It Off the Ground?" If the line drive is getting low, you should be ready to dive. Not to forget, safety should come first. If you are at risk of harm, you should not attempt to make a spectacular diving catch.

A Few Drills to Improve Your Pop-Up Skills

Make use of a fly ball machine to replicate pop-ups that are of varied heights and distances. Backpedaling, following the ball, and executing clean catches are all skills that should be practiced. To practice partner fly balls, have a team member hit fly balls with a fungo bat. This activity aims to improve your ability to communicate, track, and catch the ball at its highest point.

Juggling tennis balls can help enhance your hand-eye coordination, leading to improved tracking and catching of pop-ups.

Training Your Line Drive Reflexes to Be More Effective

Have a team member yell out directions (left, proper, straight), then hit a ground ball or line drive in the direction that was called out. This is an example of a reaction drill. Both your reaction time and your footwork will improve as a result of this workout. Use a line drive machine to replicate multiple speeds and angles of line drives. This machine is quite similar to the pop-up drill, allowing you to simulate these speeds and angles. Train yourself to track and make diving catches (while taking the necessary precautions to protect yourself). You can perform the front toss by having a team member throw line drives at you from various distances. This drill aims to improve your ability to track the ball and make a smooth catch with your Glove. You shouldn't be hesitant to ask for assistance! To avoid collisions, it is essential to communicate explicitly if a line drive is traveling toward another fielder's territory. On the field, not only is self-assurance essential, but it is also essential to be aware of your limitations.

Important Fielding Advice for a Variety of Circumstances

If a line drive travels toward the outfield wall, you should position your back against the wall and then shout for the ball. If the sun makes it difficult for you to see, you should cover your eyes with your Glove and use your peripheral vision to maintain track of the ball.

Through consistent practice of these tactics and drills, you can turn yourself from a timid outfielder into a brave fly ball chaser. You will be able to dominate the zone between first and second, transforming pop-ups into regular outs and making stunning line drive catches appear to be straightforward from your perspective. Focus, anticipation, and repetition are the three most important factors in becoming an expert at pop-ups and line drives. Now is the time to venture onto the field with self-assurance, maintain your focus on the ball, and prepare to take the skies by storm!

CHAPTER 4

OFFENSIVE CONTRIBUTIONS

Developing a consistent

"And powerful swing"

Every baseball player's ultimate desire is to hit a home run. The bat cracked against the ball, and the ball soared through the air. The ultimate source of power, however, is not only physical strength but also a consistent and repetitive swing. Developing explosive power, refining your swing technique, and transforming yourself into a striking machine can be accomplished by following these steps:

The Process of Establishing a Solid Base

A strong foundation is the first step in developing a mighty swing. When it comes to bat control and power transfer, having a stable and comfortable grip is necessary. Until you find a comfortable grip that lets you swing easily, you should try out various hand locations. Stand tall with your knees slightly bent and your weight evenly distributed on both feet. This is the correct posture. When you have a balanced posture, you have a stable base to generate power. There are several stances, but you should generally have your feet shoulder-width apart and your front foot slightly pointing in the pitcher's direction. You should select a posture that is not only comfortable but also enables you to rotate and maintain good balance.

Components that contribute to consistency

The key to hitting the ball with more consistency and solidity is to have a smooth and consistent swing. Maintain a calm position with your hands and position them just over your shoulders during the lead-up. Try not to get too worked up before the pitch is given. As soon as the pitcher begins his delivery, take a short stride with your front foot toward the pitcher. You will get momentum for your swing as a result of this. When you swing, your hips are the motor that drives it. When you swing, you should concentrate on twisting your hips in a powerful direction at the pitcher. This rotation transfers the power stored in your lower body to your upper body. Ensure that your swing plane remains level throughout the whole swing. To achieve the most significant amount of power and distance, you should strive to strike the ball squarely with the bat's sweet spot.

Developing Power

There is more to the construction of a powerful swing than merely mechanics. It is important to incorporate exercises targeting your core, legs, and shoulders when working on your strength. You may produce power for your swing by having powerful legs, shoulders, and a solid core that gives stability. Exercises, including medicine ball throws and weighted rotational training, can help you develop rotational force in your core and hips, which is essential. Practice hitting drills with lighter bats and improve bat speed using lighter bats. When you raise the speed of your bat, your hitting power will also rise.

Practice indeed makes perfect.

Dedication and constant practice are required to develop a robust and consistent swing. It is essential to practice hitting off of a tee to concentrate on your swing mechanics and your bat's path. Take things slowly at first, and as your form improves, progressively increase the speed and power of your bat. During the front toss, you should have a squad member toss you batting practice to concentrate on particular swing mechanics or hitting situations. When it comes to live pitching, nothing tops it. Getting acclimated to the pace and movement of genuine throws can be accomplished by participating in batting practice against pitchers.

Achieving Success with Self-Assurance

When it comes to power and mechanics, having a positive mental attitude is essential. Before you step up to the plate, envision yourself hitting the ball with a solid hit. This will help you achieve success. Visualizing yourself positively might help you become more focused and confident. Don't overthink your swing at the bat; try to keep a relaxed attitude. Have faith in your mechanics and concentrate on making a swing that is smooth and under control. After each game or practice, you should evaluate how well you hit the ball. List areas that could improve, and then alter your strategy accordingly.

Building a swing that is both consistent and strong is a process, not a destination in and of itself. You should continue to be committed to your practice routine, improve your technique, and increase your hitting strength. You can change yourself from a contact hitter into a batter who can turn heads with your power and consistency at the plate if you put in the effort and attention necessary throughout the process. When you take the batting stance with self-assurance, unleash the force within your swing and watch those balls soar!

Smart base running

"And stealing bases."

In a thrilling play, stealing a base is a gamble that can change the game's momentum and put your side in a position to score with a stolen base. The ability to be a smart base runner, anticipate the play, and take advantage of the vulnerabilities of the pitcher and catcher are all important aspects of the game. However, sheer speed is not the only factor that matters. The following is a guide that will help you become a master of base-stealing, leaving your opponents in a state of confusion as your team reaps the rewards:

Learn to Know Yourself

Evaluating your capabilities before attempting to steal any bases is essential. Do you have a natural high speed? Would you be able to get a solid jump on the pitcher delivery? What kind of intuition do you have when reading the pitcher and the catcher? To achieve success, being truthful about your strengths and faults is essential.

Analyzing the Current Circumstances

Attempting to steal something is not always the best course of action. When the score is close, stealing bases is more valuable than otherwise. Since the lead is comfortable, the danger may be greater than the benefit. At the beginning of the game, there are more opportunities to steal bases and develop an offensive rhythm. This is referred to as the "inning." Opportunities for thefts can be created when the pitcher has a delayed windup, a high pitch count, or a pitcher notorious for throwing to first base. Being a sluggish thrower or having a weak arm makes stealing more appealing. This is especially true for a catcher. If you have a solid hitter coming up after you, you can increase the likelihood that they will attempt to steal the ball to place them in a position to score.

The art of jumping

When it comes to a successful theft, getting a decent jump off the bag is necessary. Obtain a reasonable and lawful lead at the beginning of the procedure. Because of this, you can respond more rapidly to the pitcher's delivery. When "Keying Off the Pitcher," you should not rely just on your subconscious. To predict the throw home, it is essential to learn how to interpret the pitcher's tells, such as the leg kick or glove movement. When you take your initial step, you should explode off the bag. The throw will be more difficult to catch if you get to full speed as quickly as possible.

Communicate with your coach.

Avoid acting like a lone wolf. Have a conversation with your coach about your approach to stealing bases. They can offer insightful information regarding the pitcher, the catcher, and the general status of the game.

Here is how to make the slide

A safe slide into the base is required for a successful theft to be considered complete. This traditional slide helps you to keep in contact with the base while avoiding the tag. The Hook Slide: This slide lets you maintain contact with the base. Although this slide has the potential to be more rapid, it also carries a greater danger of damage. Utilize it in a planned manner and only when it is required. To avoid the tag, it is essential to interpret the throw as you approach the base and adjust your slide following the information you have read.

The Importance of Essential Running Fundamentals for Base Running

When it comes to stealing bases, speed is not the only factor; being a clever base runner is also essential. Running hard is something you should always do, even if you are not stealing. This puts pressure on the defense and opens the door for opportunities to steal bases later in the game.

Maintain a constant awareness of your surroundings and always be aware of where the ball is located in the game. If a ground ball is hit, you may be required to step back or move forward, depending on the circumstances. Even in situations where a steal attempt is not likely to occur, it is still possible to cause chaos by gaining a significant lead and compelling the pitcher to throw to first base. This may throw off their rhythm, leading to an opportunity to steal later. Theft of bases is a danger that is willingly taken. Stay away from becoming predictable. Use a variety of timing and base-running methods to keep the defense guessing about what you are doing. It is possible for a steal to alter the course of a game completely. But you should never put recklessness ahead of solid base running and taking a risk that has been carefully considered.

By becoming proficient in these abilities, you can convert yourself from a timid base runner into a stealthy menace to the base. You will learn to read the game, exploit its flaws, and develop into a critical attacking weapon for your side. Therefore, show some bravery and intelligence, and get ready to turn the tide of the competition with your ability to steal bases!

Bunting for hits

"And executing hit-and-runs."

Regarding baseball, hitting towering home runs is not always the focus. Sometimes, the "small ball" method is the most successful strategy. This strategy uses bunts and hit-and-runs to generate runs and fool the defense. The following guide will teach you how to become an expert in these strategizing moves, leaving your opponent's scratching their heads and your team celebrating triumphs.

The importance of precision and placement while bunting for hits

The right bunt can completely change the course of a game. Not only does it push the defense to react fast, but it also has the potential to advance runners and possibly unexpectedly hit the pitcher for a base hit. It is recommended that you adjust your bat grip to have greater control. Employ a more expansive grip while bringing your hands closer together. You should keep your weight slightly forward while maintaining a balanced stance. When the pitcher pitches, the bat face should be slightly angled downward, and the pitcher should meet the ball with the sweet spot or just below it. This is the mechanics of the bunt. Instead of striking the ball forcefully, you should concentrate on moving it in the direction you want it to go.

The ball's placement is essential; avoid bunting back to the pitcher. To make things difficult for the defense, you should aim for the infield's foul lines or soft spots. To become an expert at the bunt, you need to practice consistently. Use bunting tees, fungo bats, and teammates to practice your bunting technique and develop your ability to replicate game scenarios.

How to Execute the Hit-and-Run: The Importance of Teamwork and Timing

One of the most common strategies for the little ball is the hit-and-run. The batter intends to bunt the ball as the runner on first steals second base to increase the likelihood of a throwing error occurring and to cause confusion. Open and honest communication is essential to the success of a hit-and-run operation. After receiving the signal from the coach, the batter will then communicate it to the runner who is currently on first base. Even if it's a poor bunt, the batter needs to concentrate on making contact with the ball to be successful. Placement is also essential in this situation; you should aim for the infield grass between the pitcher and the path the base runner takes to get to second. If the pitcher is going to throw, the runner on first base needs to get a solid jump on it. When the hitter makes contact with the ball, they should immediately break for second base and take a significant lead. The squad must practice the hit-and-run, much like it is for bunting. To ensure that the execution goes smoothly, the batter and the runner need to work on improving their timing and communication.

If you want to know when to use little ball tactics,

If you have a runner on base and you need to move them into scoring position, a bunt can be a safe and trustworthy alternative for you to consider. When going up against a strong pitcher, a bunt that is executed correctly can throw off the rhythm of a dominant pitcher and establish an unexpected scoring opportunity. If the opposition side possesses a weak defensive infield and fielders that are slow, a bunt can be used to take advantage of these flaws, resulting in a base hit.

Understanding the Importance of Being Versatile

It is not enough to throw bombs to be considered a well-rounded batter. After becoming proficient in the bunt and the hit-and-run, you will become a more versatile danger at the plate. The defense is kept guessing because of this, and you can adjust your strategy according to the game's circumstances.

When it comes to small ball tactics, individual glory is not the focus; instead, the focus is on team strategy. Utilize these strategies to transform yourself into a player who can generate runs and contribute to victories in various ways, rather than only hitting home runs, and become a great asset to your team. Therefore, take the initiative with a strategy, demonstrate that you are prepared to be innovative, and demonstrate that you are an expert in the game of little ball!

CHAPTER 5

THE MENTAL GAME AT SECOND

Staying sharp

"And focused through nine innings."

Baseball is not a race; instead, it is a challenge. Keeping one's concentration and mental acuity throughout a nine-inning game is equally important as one's physical strength and hitting ability. The following is a guide that will help you develop mental endurance, maintain your energy levels, and dominate the diamond from the very first pitch to the last out:

Development Before the Game

The beginning of a successful game begins long before you even step foot on the pitch. To prepare your mind and body for optimal performance. A well-rested body is a body that is focused. Try to get a whole night's sleep before the game to ensure your mental abilities are in peak condition. To ensure that your body receives the sustained energy it needs, it is essential to fuel it with a nutritious lunch before the game. The consumption of complex carbs and lean protein can help you maintain your focus and prevent a dip in the middle of the game. Picture yourself doing well throughout the game to improve your performance. Picture yourself making firm contact with the ball, fielding ground balls without a single mistake, and maintaining your composure under intense pressure. Visualization of positive outcomes might help you feel more confident and focused. Develop a pre-game ritual that will assist you in entering the zone of performance. Getting your body and mind warmed up could involve doing things like stretching, listening to music, or performing some mild swings.

Preserving One's Concentration Throughout the Action

Active effort is required to maintain mental sharpness over the entire nine innings. Don't worry about the future or concentrate on mistakes you've made in the past; instead, stay in the here and now. Only focus on the situation that is occurring right now, which includes the pitch that is now being played and the play that is taking place on the field. You should silence your inner critic by engaging in positive self-talk. Alternately, replace negative ideas with good affirmations. Visualize yourself succeeding and remind yourself of the skills and capabilities you possess. Taking slow, deep breaths under control can assist you in managing stress and keeping your attention on the task at hand. To calm your anxieties and clear your mind before each pitch, take a few deep breaths and focus on breathing. Keeping yourself hydrated is essential since dehydration can cause weariness and reduce focus. Continue to drink water throughout the game to ensure you remain hydrated and keep your mental and physical performance at its peak. Construct a mental "anchor" that you may return to whenever you feel your concentration beginning to waver. This could be a particular word, a visualization, or a physical movement that assists you in refocusing your attention on the here and now.

Maintaining Your Energy for the Long Game

Physical stamina is also required for a struggle that lasts for nine innings. Bring nutritious snacks to snack on as you watch the game. A short energy boost that does not leave a heavy sensation can be obtained from foods such as fruits, almonds, and granola bars. Maintaining proper hydration is essential. It is impossible to place enough emphasis on this particular point. Consuming water regularly guarantees that both your body and mind are operating at their optimal level. During breaks, moving around and avoiding being stationary on the bench is essential. You should engage in some light jogging, dynamic stretching, or light throwing during the inning breaks to maintain a relaxed and alert state of mind. To maintain a great team environment, it is essential to surround oneself with positive teammates and coaches who can elevate your spirits and push you during the game.

Recovering from errors is an essential component of mental toughness.

Errors are a part of the game of baseball. Even the most skilled athletes hit a home run or commit an error. I have a short memory, so I try not to dwell on my mistakes. Learn from them but give them up as soon as possible. Keep your attention on the next pitch, the next play, and the chance to make amends for your past mistakes. After each inning, you should analyze your at-bats to learn from each one. What did you find to be successful? How could you have handled the situation differently? You will be able to enhance your focus and performance in future at-bats by learning from your experiences and applying what you have learned. Give yourself credit for the things you've accomplished!

A moment of celebration is justifiable for any of the following: a fantastic catch, a decent hit, or a strikeout. Thanks to this positive reinforcement, your self-assurance will remain strong throughout the game.

Practice is the best way to acquire the ability to maintain concentration and energy over the entire nine innings of a game. You can change yourself from a player who loses steam late in games into a mental powerhouse prepared to dominate for all nine innings by prioritizing pre-game preparation, utilizing strategies that help you focus, maintaining your energy levels, and fostering mental toughness. To triumph over the long haul, you should enter the field with a concentrated mind and a determined spirit.

Handling errors

"And maintaining confidence."

The game of baseball is played in inches. Errors may be pretty disheartening, and they can be caused by anything from a wayward throw to a failed catch to a ground ball that is evaluated incorrectly. However, even the most skilled players can make errors. To achieve success, it is not necessary to avoid them altogether; instead, acquiring the skills required to deal with them and recover confidence is essential. Those moments of frustration can be transformed into chances for growth if you follow these steps:

Recognizing and Accepting Responsibility

Acknowledging the mistake is the first step in the process. Not attempt to shift responsibility or concentrate on the situation. Accept responsibility for the error and make an effort to improve. Examine the causes of the problem. You got the trajectory of the ball wrong, didn't you? Is your footwork not up to par? You will be able to avoid making errors of a similar nature in the future if you uncover the source.

Recognize and Embrace Your Short Memory

Baseball is a fast-paced sport. Dwelling on your error will not affect the play that has already taken place, and it may hurt your performance in the future. Get rid of it. Pay attention to the next pitch, the next chance to redeem yourself, and the next opportunity. Maintain your composure and focus on the task at hand since your teammates depend on you.

Look for Assistance

Don't keep your feelings bottled up inside. You should discuss how you feel with your coach, a team member, or a friend you can rely on. Because of their point of view, you will be able to comprehend the error and regain your trust.

Learn from the Past's Greatest Figures

Every single one of the best players makes mistakes. Take note of how people respond. Typically, they admit that they made a mistake, adjust their strategy, and then return with a stronger mindset. Utilize these instances from real life to motivate and inspire your resiliency.

Talking to Oneself in a Positive Manner

The voice that you hear within yourself can be your most ardent supporter or your harshest critic. Put a stop to the negative talk. Alternately, replace negative ideas with good affirmations. Make sure you are aware of your abilities and previous achievements. Imagine that you can execute the play flawlessly when the next opportunity presents itself.

Put your attention on the things that you can control

Although you cannot influence the results of every play, you can manage your level of effort, attitude, and concentration. You should focus on these things and have faith in your capabilities.

Practice indeed makes perfect.

Inadequate preparation is frequently the root cause of errors. Enhance your abilities by participating in practice sessions. Fielding drills, footwork workouts, and throwing mechanics are all critical areas to focus on. Gaining a better understanding of the fundamentals can help you become a more self-assured and dependable player.

Honor and Commemorate Your Achievements

Do not allow mistakes to overshadow the achievements you have achieved. Recognize your successes, no matter how big or how tiny they may be. Whether it be a decent at-bat, a strong throw, or a beautiful grab, all these things deserve a moment of positivity. Rewarding oneself for these accomplishments helps one feel more confident and reinforces beneficial habits.

Put your attention on the team.

One of the team sports is baseball. Keep in mind that you are not the only one out there. If you make a mistake, your teammates will be there to cheer you on and help you pick yourself up. Pay attention to how you can contribute to the team's success, and your self-assurance will automatically increase as you assist your team in achieving victory.

Mistakes will inevitably be made in this game. Don't let them establish who you are. By handling them with maturity, learning from them, and maintaining a good attitude, you'll change from a player who buckles under pressure to a resilient competitor, ready to bounce back stronger and contribute to your team's victory. Keep your head up, take the lessons you've learned from your past blunders, and go into the following play with renewed confidence!

Being a vocal leader

"In the infield"

The infield consists of fielding grounders, turning double plays, and other things. A loud leader on the infield can distinguish between a chaotic disaster and a well-oiled machine. The infield is the heart of the defense, and someone vocal can make all the difference. Developing your leadership abilities, becoming the defensive anchor, and making your presence known on the diamond may be accomplished by following these four steps:

"Lead by Example"

Instead of words, actions speak far louder. Be the kind of player that makes your teammates want to follow in your footsteps before you start giving directions. After every ball, you should put in much effort during practice and maintain a positive attitude while on the field. When you demonstrate dedication and commitment by your actions, the words that you put forward will have more weight.

Be familiar with the game.

A strong leader is someone who is entirely familiar with the game. Research the hitters, scrutinize their tendencies, and try to anticipate the scenarios. Having the ability to read the pitcher, the count, and the baserunners is essential. Because you have this expertise, you can call the appropriate plays at the appropriate times, instilling trust in your players.

Communicate Clearly and Concisely

You won't be considered a leader if you shout out directions at random. Develop your ability to communicate clearly and succinctly. Make a decisive call on the cutoffs, announce the possibility of double plays, and convey any revisions to placement based on the circumstances. Instead of yelling unnecessarily, speak loudly enough to be heard above the crowd, but avoid doing so.

Maintain a positive and encouraging attitude.

A genuine leader is someone who helps others succeed. Being the first person to celebrate with a teammate after they have made a tremendous play is essential. Please provide words of support and encouragement after you have made a mistake. Creating a happy environment boosts the team's morale and encourages everyone to perform to the best of their abilities.

Discover Who Your Teammates Are

Individually, each player is unique. Take into account both the talents and shortcomings of your teammates. Whenever it is necessary, provide criticism that is specific and helpful, but make sure to do so in a manner that is both respectful and encouraging.

Lead by Position"

You are the captain of the defense team. Manage the pitchers, call the pitches, and control the tempo of the game and the game itself. As you communicate with the umpire, pitcher, and infielders, be vocal with your signs and maintain open lines of communication. You should serve as a vocal anchor on the right side of the infield. Communicate with the runners on base and direct throws emanating from the outfield. Your poise and self-assurance can potentially establish the tone for the infield. You will be the quarterback for the infield. You are responsible for supervising the middle infield, calling cutoffs, and coordinating plays with the shortstop. Your ability to communicate and familiarity with the game are pretty important. It is you who is the rover. Make sure to communicate your positioning following the hitter and the circumstances. Prepare yourself to make plays on bunts, line drives, and throw runners out at home so that you can score.

Lead by Situation

With two outs, it is essential to emphasize making the out, even if doing so requires you to forego a clean play in favor of a quicker throw. It is necessary to communicate the possibilities of double play and to have everyone in position. It is required to call cutoffs and be outspoken about potential plays at the plate when there are currently runners on base. Keeping your teammates informed about possible baserunners and efforts to steal is essential.

Commanding others is not the essence of leadership; it instills trust and confidence in others. You may change from a single infielder into a vocal leader who commands respect and directs your team to defensive domination by adopting the appropriate mentality, becoming an expert in the game, and effectively communicating with your teammates. Therefore, take the field with the mindset of a leader, make your voice heard, and become the defensive pillar your team requires!

CHAPTER 6

TRAINING AND PREPARATION

Effective practice routines

"And drills for second basemen."

It is not enough to catch grounders at second base and flip the ball to first base. Owning the middle infield, anticipating plays, and making acrobatic catches appear routine are all essential aspects of this game. Your transformation into a second base maestro can be accomplished by following these steps to create a winning practice regimen that is packed with drills:

The Process of Establishing a Solid Base

The development of footwork routines that are both swift and smooth is a priority. Becoming proficient in shuffling from side to side, back pedaling, and lunging explosively towards ground balls is essential. Fielding grounders begin with a good glove posture, emphasizing glove work's importance. Catching balls with a soft hand and quickly transferring them to your throwing hand should be part of your routine. The mechanics of throwing include developing a throwing motion that is both powerful and accurate. Pay attention to the correct mechanics of your arms, a decisive engagement of your core, and a clean follow-through.

Exercises that Help You Improve Your Skills

Have a teammate hit ground balls from a variety of angles and distances. Prioritize cleanly fielding the ball and producing rapid and accurate throws. Use a ground ball machine to imitate various speeds and spins applied to grounders. Because of this, you can respond rapidly and make decisions in a split second. A coach can hit fungo grounders to replicate bunts or high-chopper sequences. By practicing, develop your ability to field these tricky bounces and make the appropriate throw.

Use a fly ball machine to practice tracking fly balls and making diving catches. If you begin at lower speeds, gradually raise the problem's difficulty. Instruct a team member to hit fly balls of varied heights and weights. Focus on reading the ball as it comes off the bat, calling for the ball if it is required, and completing a seamless catch. Work on your ability to track fly balls that have been hit against an outfield wall by practicing wall drills. To catch a catch, you must backpedal and time your jump correctly. This will replicate those conditions. To practice turning double plays, you should work in pairs with a shortstop and a first baseman; this will help you improve your skills. Put your attention on communicating effectively, transitioning quickly, and throwing accurately. By having a partner throw from various distances, you may simulate relay throws from the outfield using this technique. Get some practice catching the ball while you're running and throwing it to first base with a lot of force. In the situational drills, you will simulate steal attempts with a runner on first base. In the steal attempts drill, you will simulate steal attempts. Your footwork throws to the plate, and communication with the catcher should all be practiced. You should practice fielding bunts and making rapid throws to first or home to improve your bunt defense, depending on the circumstances.

The Process of Developing Your Practice Routine

You should start each practice session with a dynamic warm-up to get your body ready for movement. Determine your areas of weakness and devote some of your time to drills that target those areas. Avoid becoming mired down in a rut! Keeping your practice sessions enjoyable and productive requires switching up the drills you do. Visualization is an effective weapon. Visualize yourself being able to do a drill without any mistakes before you try it.

What's Beyond the Drills

Identify areas for improvement by analyzing the game tape. If you want to learn new tactics, watch professional second basemen. It is crucial to have a strong core and an upper body. Make sure that your routine includes activities that focus on strength training.

Dedication and persistent practice are required to achieve the status of second base star. Immerse yourself in the grind, become an expert in the fundamentals, and hone your talents using tailored drills. Do not hesitate to try new things, ask for criticism from your coaches, and, most importantly, enjoy yourself while on the field. Through consistent effort and applying the appropriate strategy, you can turn yourself from a raw talent into a second baseman who commands respect and dominates the middle infield.

Strength and conditioning

"Tailored for the position"

The second base is a position that calls for a unique combination of agility, power, and stability. You need a training regimen catering to these particular requirements to dominate the middle infield position genuinely. To become a defensive force and a menace on the base paths, here is how you may customize your strength and conditioning routine to meet your fitness needs:

The Process of Establishing a Solid Base

To maintain stability and explosiveness, it is necessary to have a rock-solid core. You can respond swiftly and execute strong throws by engaging your core muscles with exercises such as planks, side planks, and Russian twists. Having strong legs is necessary to drive off the ground for throws and cover ground in the infield. It is possible to improve lower body power by performing squats, lunges, and box jumps. This will enable you to surge at grounders and make rapid throws to first. Take care of your upper body! Strengthening your throwing arm and improving your bat speed can be accomplished through push-ups, rows, and overhead presses.

Increasing Your Capacity for Agility and Quickness

Individuals who play second base must move fast from side to side. You can enhance your footwork and ability to quickly change directions by practicing lateral shuffles with cones or agility ladders. Activities such as box jumps and jump squats are examples of plyometric exercises. These exercises will help you develop explosive power, enabling you to react and get to ground balls more quickly. You can enhance your reaction time and agility by practicing drills that imitate game circumstances, such as shifting directions to chase down a ground ball or retreating for a fly ball. These drills are referred to as "change of direction drills."

Movement and endurance

Becoming a threat on the base paths requires speed, which is why sprints are so important. To improve your ability to steal bases and run the bases efficiently, you should incorporate sprints of varied distances into your practice. These sprints should include both short bursts and extended runs. Interval training helps increase stamina, which is essential for consistently performing at a high level over a long game. While you are working to build your cardiovascular endurance, you should alternate between periods of high-intensity exercise and intervals of recovery.

Listen to your body and give yourself enough time to relax and recover. If you combine a nutritious diet with a comprehensive strength and conditioning program, you will be able to fuel your performance and reduce the likelihood of hurting yourself. By implementing this individualized program, you can turn yourself from a competent second baseman into a formidable force on the sporting field. Because of your power, agility, and stamina, you can make plays appear effortless, maintain control of the middle infield, and leave opposing batters and base runners in disbelief!

Scouting reports

"Game preparation and strategic planning"

You must do more than just hit a bat and catch a ball to play baseball. It's like chess in your head between leaders and players. To get ahead of the competition, it's essential to learn scouting reports, carefully prepare for games, and plan strategically. Here's how to go from being a passive player to a genius of strategy:

Scouting Reports: Your Look at the Other Team

Scouting reports give you information about the other team. They describe player patterns, look at pitching styles, and find possible weaknesses. You should carefully read the spy reports before every game to "Know Your Enemy." Learn how the other team's batters approach their pitches, what pitches they have trouble with, and how often they tend to run the bases. Check out the pitcher's fastball velocity, breaking ball types, and favorite hitting zones. Look for patterns in the way they tend to pitch. Visual support works very well. Watch the other team's game film and how the batters and pitchers hit and throw the ball.

Getting Ready for the Game: Sharpening Your Tools

Getting ready is essential for doing your best on game day. Do drills that are like real games. To make fungo bats that look like fly balls, work on double-play turns with your partners and steal bases against a catcher. Talk with your friends about the coach's plan before the game. Learn how to set up your defense, how to run the bases, and what might happen in different situations. Mental practice is beneficial. Picture yourself making good contact with the ball, executing double plays flawlessly, and implementing essential defense plays.

Strategic Planning: Making Changes on the Spot

During a game, even the best-planned plans can change. Here's how to change your plan depending on what's going on:

Make changes based on the pitcher: Watch how the player changes as the game progresses. Change how you hit by focusing on hitting for contact instead of power or looking for specific pitches.

Make the most of your weaknesses: Did you notice that a batter had trouble with a specific pitch? Let your thrower or catcher know this. Take advantage of flaws to get ahead.

Think Like a Coach: You should be like the coach on the field. You are learning to recognize when a bunt or a stolen base could be helpful. Tell your friends about possible strategies.

Scouting reports, game planning, and making strategy plans are all done together. Talk to your coaches and peers transparently. You can turn your team from a group of people into a strategic unit ready to beat any opponent if you all work together.

Closing Thoughts

The path of baseball is more than just a game; it's a way to learn, plan, and work together. This e-book has given you the information and tools to improve your skills as a player, whether you're good at stealing bases, playing defense, or planning. Baseball is a sport that you can continually improve. Take on the tasks, consider what went wrong, and enjoy your wins. Enjoy yourself most of all! What makes baseball great are the friends you make, the thrill of the game, and the satisfaction of getting better at it. Go confidently on the field, use what you've learned, and make your mark on the game. Don't forget that getting better at baseball is a process that never ends. This e-book is just the start. Go out there, work hard at practice, and show everyone what you can do!